First World War
and Army of Occupation
War Diary
France, Belgium and Germany

57 DIVISION
171 Infantry Brigade
King's (Liverpool Regiment)
2/5 Battalion
11 February 1917 - 31 January 1918

WO95/2983/2

The Naval & Military Press Ltd
www.nmarchive.com
Published in association with The National Archives

Published by

The Naval & Military Press Ltd

Unit 10 Ridgewood Industrial Park,

Uckfield, East Sussex,

TN22 5QE England

Tel: +44 (0) 1825 749494

www.naval-military-press.com

www.nmarchive.com

This diary has been reprinted in facsimile from the original. Any imperfections are inevitably reproduced and the quality may fall short of modern type and cartographic standards.

© Crown Copyright
Images reproduced by permission of The National Archives, London, England, 2015.

Contents

Document type	Place/Title	Date From	Date To
Heading	WO95/2983/2 57Div 171 Infantry Bde 2/5 Btn Kings Liverpool Regt Feb 1917-Jan 1918		
War Diary		11/02/1917	20/02/1917
War Diary	La Boutillerie	21/02/1917	28/02/1917
Miscellaneous	War Diary For The Month Of March	03/04/1917	03/04/1917
War Diary	La Boutillerie	01/03/1917	01/03/1917
War Diary	Fleurbaix	02/03/1917	08/03/1917
War Diary	Erquingham	09/03/1917	20/03/1917
War Diary	Bois Grenier	28/03/1917	31/03/1917
Miscellaneous	Herewith War Diary Of This Unit for The month Of April 1917	04/05/1917	04/05/1917
War Diary	Bois Grenier	01/04/1917	30/04/1917
War Diary	L'Epinnete	01/05/1917	03/05/1917
War Diary	Armentieres	04/05/1917	11/05/1917
War Diary	L'Epinnete Sub-Sector	12/05/1917	21/05/1917
War Diary	Armentieres	22/05/1917	29/05/1917
War Diary	L'Epinnete-Sub-Sector	30/05/1917	31/05/1917
War Diary	L'Epinnete Sub-Sector	01/06/1917	08/06/1917
War Diary	Armentieres	09/06/1917	16/06/1917
War Diary	L'Epinnete Sub-Sector	17/06/1917	24/06/1917
War Diary	Armentieres	25/06/1917	30/06/1917
Heading	War Diary Of 2/5th Bn The Kings For July 1917 Missing		
Miscellaneous	2/5th Kings Liverpool Regt		
War Diary	Bac-St-Maun	01/08/1917	03/08/1917
War Diary	Ronge de Bont	04/08/1917	07/08/1917
War Diary	Cordonnerie	08/08/1917	16/08/1917
War Diary	Rouge De Bout	19/08/1917	23/08/1917
War Diary	Cordonnerie	24/08/1917	27/08/1917
Miscellaneous	War Diary For The Month Of September	30/09/1917	30/09/1917
War Diary	Cordonnerie	09/09/1917	19/09/1917
War Diary	St Hilaire	20/09/1917	25/10/1917
War Diary	Eagle Trench U23.c.90.90 Bixchoote 205. W.4	26/10/1917	28/10/1917
War Diary	Huddleson Camp D.7.B Central St Julien 28.N.W.2	29/10/1917	30/10/1917
War Diary	Marsouin Farm C.8.B.60.10 St Julien 28 N.W.2	31/10/1917	31/10/1917
Miscellaneous	2/5th The Kings Liverpool In The Field	30/11/1917	30/11/1917
War Diary	Marsouin Farm (St. Julien 28.N.W.2 C 8 B.60.10)	01/11/1917	01/11/1917
War Diary	Eagle Trench U.23 C.90.90	01/11/1917	02/11/1917
War Diary	Wolff Camp	03/11/1917	06/11/1917
War Diary	La Panne	16/11/1917	01/12/1917
War Diary	Proven	08/12/1917	16/12/1917
War Diary	Boesinghe	17/12/1917	25/12/1917
War Diary	Elverdinghe	29/12/1917	29/12/1917
War Diary	Proven	30/12/1917	30/12/1917
War Diary	Meteren	31/12/1917	31/12/1917
War Diary	Armentieres	01/01/1918	21/01/1918
Miscellaneous	2/qurs kings Lpool Rgt In the field 1.2.1918	01/02/1918	01/02/1918
War Diary	Armentieres	24/01/1918	31/01/1918

WO 95/2983/2

57 DIV
171 INFANTRY BDE

2/5 Bn KINGS LIVERPOOL REGT
Feb 1917 - Jan 1918

WAR DIARY
or
INTELLIGENCE SUMMARY.
(Erase heading not required.)

Army Form C. 2118.

2/5 Liverpool R.
Vol I

1.'O'.
(8 sheets)

Instructions regarding War Diaries and Intelligence
Summaries are contained in F. S. Regs., Part II.
and the Staff Manual respectively. Title pages
will be prepared in manuscript.

Place	Date	Hour	Summary of Events and Information	Remarks and references to Appendices
	1917			
	11 Feb.		Transport left SOUTHAMPTON for HAVRE.	
	13 Feb.	10.20 a.m.	Battalion embarked from FOLKESTONE.	
		12.5 p.m.	Battalion disembarked at BOULOGNE and marched to Ostrehove Rest Camp.	
	14 Feb.	8.30am	Battalion less 3 platoons entrained at BOULOGNE	
		9.30pm	- do - arrived at BAILLEUL, marched to & billeted at STRAZEELE.	
	15 Feb.	11.30pm	Remainder of Battalion arrived at STRAZEELE. Transport arrived.	
	16 Feb.		Training at STRAZEELE.	
	17 Feb.		Training at STRAZEELE.	
	18 Feb.		Training at STRAZEELE.	
	19 Feb.		Training at STRAZEELE. Billeting party left for SAILLY.	
	20 Feb.	8.25am	Battalion marched to & billeted at SAILLY.	
LA BOUTILLERIE	21 Feb.	12 noon	Battalion took over right sub-sector of trenches LA BOUTILLERIE from 1st Batt. Wellington Infantry Regiment.	
- do -	22 Feb.		In the trenches. One casualty.(WKKK killed)	
- do -	23 Feb.		- do -	
- do -	24 Feb.		- do - One casualty.(wounded)	

O.C. 2/5th Bn. "The King's" (L'pool Regt.)
Lieut Col.

WAR DIARY
INTELLIGENCE SUMMARY.

Army Form C. 2118.

Place	Date	Hour	Summary of Events and Information	Remarks and references to Appendices
	1917			
LA BOUTILLERIE	25 Feb.		In the trenches.	
- do -	26 Feb.		- do - Four casualties. (Wounded)	
- do -	27 Feb.		- do -	
- do -	28 Feb.		- do - Seven casualties. (3 killed, 4 wounded)	

MacIver
Lieut. Col.
O.C. 2/5th Btn. "The King's" (L'pool Regt.)

SECRET. April 1st.17.   N/14

To. Officer l/c.
    Northern Section.

                                    original
        I enclose herewith the ~~duplicate~~ of this unit's
War Diary for the month of March.

                                L.W.Statt. Capt & adjutant
                                            for
                                Lieut.Colonel
                Commanding 2/5th.Bn."The King's"'L'pool Regt.

        Officer i/c War Diaries
            G.H.Q. 3rd Echelon.

        Herewith, please acknowledge receipt.

                    E.T.Woodley. Major.
3-4-17.   Off. i/c S. Inf. Northern Section

Army Form C. 2118.

2/5 Liverpool Regt
Vol 2

WAR DIARY
or
INTELLIGENCE SUMMARY
(Erase heading not required.)

Place	Date	Hour	Summary of Events and Information	Remarks and references to Appendices
	March			
LA BOUTILLERIE	1	8am	Relieved by 2/8th K.L.R. Battalion went into Divisional reserve in FLEURBAIX.	R.
FLEURBAIX	2		In billets in FLEURBAIX. Provided working parties for maintenance and improvement of trenches and roads in rear.	H.
- do -	3		- do -	H.
- do -	4		- do -	R.
- do -	5		- do -	R.
- do -	6		- do -	R.
- do -	7		- do - Batt. became Brigade reserve in same billets.	R.
- do -	8.10am		Received orders to move to billets in FORT ROMPU.	R.
- do -	8		Moved into temporary billets in ERQUINGHEM, FORT ROMPU area not being available.	R.
ERQUINGHEM	9	8am	Battalion took over billets of 2/10th K.L.R. on RUE DELPIERRE	R.
- do -	10		All companies training.	R.
- do -	11 to 17		Specialists training. Remainder of Batt. providing working parties by day, reclaiming and wiring subsidiary line, maintaining and improving Communication trenches.	R.
- do -	18 to 27		Specialists training. Remainder of Batt. providing working parties by night, wiring and draining subsidiary line.	R.
- do -	20		Two companies attended a lecture and demonstration of anti-gas shell precautions.	R.

Army Form C. 2118.

WAR DIARY
or
INTELLIGENCE SUMMARY.
(Erase heading not required.)

Instructions regarding War Diaries and Intelligence Summaries are contained in F. S. Regs., Part II. and the Staff Manual respectively. Title pages will be prepared in manuscript.

Place	Date	Hour	Summary of Events and Information	Remarks and references to Appendices
	March			
BOIS GRENIER.	28	10am	Took over BOIS GRENIER sector of trenches from 2/9th K.L.R. Casualties, 2 killed, 1 wounded.	A
" do "	29		In trenches. Casualties. One officer killed. 2nd Lt. C.M.Hudson. 1 O.R. killed, 1 wounded.	A
" do "	30		In trenches.	A
" do "	31		In trenches.	A

M Manley Cohen .... Lt. Col.
Commanding 2/5th K.L.R.

T2134. Wt. W708-776. 50C090. 4/15. Sir J. C. & S.

May 4th. 1917.

To. D.A.G.
   3rd.Echelon. B.E.F.

I enclose herewith War Diary of this unit for the month of April 1917.

[signature] Lieut.Colonel
Cdg.2/5th.Bn.King'sm,L'pool Regiment.

WAR DIARY
or
~~INTELLIGENCE SUMMARY.~~
(Erase heading not required.)

Army Form C. 2118.

2/5 Liverpool Regt
Part 3

Place	Date	Hour	Summary of Events and Information	Remarks and references to Appendices
BOIS GRENIER XXXXXXX	1.4.17 to 4.4.17		In trenches BOIS GRENIER sector. Strength of unit, 39 officers, 885 O.R.	
	5.4.17	8.15pm	Batt. less B Company relieved by 2/8th K.L.R. Took over right Brigade reserve.	
	6.4.17 to 11.4.17		B Company remained in Subsidary line under O.C. 2/8th K.L.R. In Brigade reserve, specialists training, remainder of Batt. finding working parties in BOIS GRENIER sector	
	12.4.17		Relieved in right Brigade sector by 2/9th K.L.R. and went into Divisional Reserve at Bac St. Maur, taking over billets of 2/10th. K.L.R.	
	13.4.17 to 23.4.17		In Divisional reserve, found working parties for the trenches & permanent fatigue party at STRAZEELE.	
	24.4.17	1.30pm	Moved into billets in ARMENTIERES, preparatory to taking over new sector.	
		6.00pm	Advance parties from Companies and all Lewis Guns went into trenches.	
	25.4.17	8.00pm	Batt. took over EPINETTE sector from 10th Australian Infantry Brigade.	
	26.4.17 to 30.4.17		In trenches. Night of 28/29th. Gas released from our sector in conjunction with Brigade on our left. Result not known, no retaliation on our sector. Strength 46 officers 871 O.R.	

WAR DIARY or INTELLIGENCE SUMMARY

Army Form C. 2118.

2/5 Liverpool

Place	Date	Hour	Summary of Events and Information	Remarks and references to Appendices
	MAY.		STRENGTH 47 officers 868 O.R.	
L'EPINNETTE	1		In trenches (L'EPINNETE sub-sector) Enemy artillery registering continuously. Cas:1 O.R.killed	
"	2		- do - - do -	
"	3	9.p.m.	Relieved by 2/8th K.L.R. completed by 11.50 p.m. Went into Right Brigade reserve in ARMENTIERES "D" Company remained in Subsidiary Line under 2/8th K.L.R. Lewis Guns relieved at daybreak on morning of 4th.	
ARMENTIERES	4		In Brigade reserve. "A", "B", & "C" Coys. and specialists training	
"	5 & 6		- do - - do -	
"	7		- do - Enemy raid on L'EPINNETE, HOUPLINES sector 8.30.p.m. Battalion ordered to "Stand by". 9p.m. "C" Company re-inforced Bett. in the line.	
"		8.40pm 10.40pm	Whole of 2nd Army guns fired 5 shots. ARMENTIERES lightly shelled in retaliation of 2nd shoot. Casualties 1 officer & 2 O.R's wounded	
"	8		In Brigade reserve. Coys. and specialists training. Casualties. 1 O.R. killed.1 died of wounds 3 wounded. (caused through working party of company in the line being shelled.)	
"	9		In Brigade reserve. Casualties 20.B. killed 5 wounded.	
"	10		- do - Received orders for relief of 2/8th K.L.R. 9p.m. Lewis Guns moved into Subsidiary line & relieved 2/8th L.Gs. at daybreak on 11th. Casualties 10.R. died of wounds.	
"	11	9pm	Commenced relief of 2/8th K.L.R. in EPINNETE sub-sector. Relief complete 11.30 p.m.	

Army Form C. 2118.

WAR DIARY
or
INTELLIGENCE SUMMARY.
(Erase heading not required.)

Instructions regarding War Diaries and Intelligence Summaries are contained in F.S. Regs., Part II. and the Staff Manual respectively. Title pages will be prepared in manuscript.

Place	Date	Hour	Summary of Events and Information	Remarks and references to Appendices
L'EPINETTE sub-sector	May 12		In trenches. Enemy artillery searching for battery positions during morning, otherwise quiet.	
"	13		- do - - do - - do - all day	
"	14 to 20.		- do - Enemy attitude extremely quiet.	
"			Gas cylinders installed in front line between 17th & 19th. Casualties. 16th 2 O.R. wounded. 19th 3 O.R. wounded. 20th 2 O.R. wounded	
"	21.	9.15pm	Relief by 2/8th K.L.R. commenced, complete 11.45pm "A" Company remained in Subsidiary line under 2/8th. Lewis Guns relieved at daybreak on 22nd. Battalion went into Right Brigade Reserve in ARMENTIERES.	
ARMENTIERES.	22 to 27.		In Brigade reserve. Coys and specialists training.	
"	25		"C" Company relieved "A" Company in subsidiary line of L'EPINETTE sub-sector	
"	28		Orders for relief of 2/8th K.L.R. received. 8pm. Lewis Guns went into subsidiary line and relieved 2/8th L.Gs. at daybreak on 29th.	
"	29		Relief of 2/8th cancelled owing to possible discharge of Gas from L'EPINETTE sub-sector.	
"	30	9.15pm	Relief of 2/8th K.L.R. commenced, complete 12.5 am	
EPINETTE sub-sector	31		In trenches. Enemy attitude fairly quiet.	

STRENGTH OF BATTALION 45 OFFICERS 825 O. R.

[signature] Lieut. Colonel.
Commanding 2/5th. K. L. R.

WAR DIARY
or
INTELLIGENCE SUMMARY.

(Erase heading not required.)

Army Form C. 2118.

Place	Date	Hour	Summary of Events and Information	Remarks and references to Appendices
L'EPINNETE sub-sector	June 1		STRENGTH. 45 officers, 825 O.R. In trenches.	CASUALTIES. 1 O.R. killed. 2 wounded
"	2		- do -	"
"	3		- do -	1 OR " 5 "
"	4		- do -	"
"	5		- do -	2 "
"	6		- do -	"
"	7		- do - Received orders for relief, which was postponed owing to proposed raid on enemy trenches, and discharge of gas. These were afterwards cancelled.	2 " 1 "
"	8	9.15pm.	Relief by 2/8th. K.L.R. commenced. Relief complete 11.40pm. "A" company remained Batt. in subsidiary line under orders of 2/8th. K.L.R. Went into right reserve in ARMENTIERES	4 "
ARMENTIERES	9		In billets. 250 men on working and wiring parties in trenches (L'EPINNETE)	1 O.R. died of wounds 1 O.R. "
"	10		- do -	
"	11		- do - Batt. stood to in billets owing to hostile raid on HOUPLINES sub-sector, no further action taken.	1 wounded

J/M/Leyton
Lt. Colonel, Commanding.
2/5th K.L.R.

Army Form C. 2118.

WAR DIARY
or
INTELLIGENCE SUMMARY.
(Erase heading not required.)

Instructions regarding War Diaries and Intelligence Summaries are contained in F.S. Regs., Part II. and the Staff Manual respectively. Title pages will be prepared in manuscript.

Place	Date	Hour	Summary of Events and Information	Remarks and references to Appendices
				CASUALTIES
ARMENTIERES.	June.12		In billets. 250 men on wiring and working parties in the trenches. "B" Company relieved "A" company in the subsidiary line	6 OR.wounded
"	13		In billets. Working and wiring parties cancelled owing to gas discharge which was ~~again cancelled~~ took place at 12.30 am 14th.	
"	14		In billets. Working and wiring parties as previously.	1 OR wounded
"	15		- do - - do -	1 OR killed 2 "
"	16	9.30pm	- do - commenced relief of 2/8th K.L.R. in L'EPINNETE sub sector.	
		11.55pm	Relief complete. ARMENTIERES was shelled every day between 9th and 16th, chiefly between 1030 & 11.30 pm and 2 & 3 am.	
L'EPINNETE sub sector.	17		In trenches. No unusual activity.	1 OR wounded
"	18 to 24		" Enemy artillery far more active than usual, all types of arms being used. Registration was noticed on all C.T's, the front line and support line. This resulted on the morning of the 24th in an attempted raid on our trenches. At 2.10 am a heavy barrage was opened on our line (36NW I5c to I10d) soon after, an enemy party were seen in No Mens Land (II.1c) which failed to reach our lines. All quiet at 3.am.	21st. 3 " 22nd 2 " 24th 1 officer,2OR killed 6 O R wounded

W. Malyhen
Lt. Colonel, Commanding
2/5th. K.L.R.

T/134. Wt. W708-776. 500000. 4/15. Sir J.C. & S.

Army Form C. 2118.

WAR DIARY
or
INTELLIGENCE SUMMARY.
(Erase heading not required.)

Instructions regarding War Diaries and Intelligence Summaries are contained in F. S. Regs., Part II. and the Staff Manual respectively. Title pages will be prepared in manuscript.

Place	Date	Hour	Summary of Events and Information	Remarks and references to Appendices
L'EPINETTE sub sector.	June 24	9.45pm	Relief by 2/8th K.L.R. commenced, completed 12.10am. Battalion went into right reserve in ARMENTIERES. "C" company remained in subsidiary line under orders of 2/8th K.L.R.	
ARMENTIERES	25		In billets. 250 men on working and wiring parties in trenches. Specialists training	
"	26.		— do — Working and wiring parties cancelled owing to proposed gas operations which were cancelled. Specialists training.	
"	27.		In billets. 250 men on working and wiring parties in trenches. Specialists training	
"	28		— do — — do — Casuality 1 O.R. wounded	
"	29		9.45pm "D" Company relieved "C" Company in subsidiary line. In billets. Working and wiring parties as previously	
"	30		— do — — do — 1 O.R. missing Received 9 reinforcements from base.	
			STRENGTH. 42 officers 753 O. R.	

J. Mailyler
Lt. Colonel. Commanding
2/5th K.L.R.

War Diary
of
2/5th Bn.
The Kings, for
July 1917,
missing

Yves, east of Ploegsteert Wood. Two houses and some trenches were captured, but the attackers then found themselves held up by machine-gun fire and wire, and, as it was found impossible to consolidate, as the trenches filled with water as fast as they were dug, and to build up breast-works[K.] in the open was impossible,* the attack was

---
* A breastwork is a parapet built above ground, with earth excavated from a trench, usually in front.
---

abandoned on the 25th, and the original line, on higher ground, was re-occupied.

The German retaliation for the Allied offensive came on the 20th, and, as usual, against the weak spot in the line. At daylight on that day the whole front of the Indian Corps was bombarded by heavy artillery and trench mortars. At 9 a.m. some mines were exploded in front of Givenchy. These preliminaries were followed up by infantry attacks, with much bombing, on Givenchy and the front

To.
2/Lt Winn
    Adjutant
      2/5th Kings Liverpool Regt.

Herewith War Diary for August in accordance with D.R.O. 667 dated 22.5.17.

R.W.B Page 2Lt.
   for Adjutant
      2/5th K.L.R.

WAR DIARY or INTELLIGENCE SUMMARY

Army Form C. 2118.

Place	Date	Hour	Summary of Events and Information	Remarks and references to Appendices
Bac St Maur	1/8/17	4.30 am	The Battalion under Capt H.S. Read arrived at Bac-St-maur in the early morning took over Billets Here. The Headquarters of the 2/5th KLR & the 2/6th K.L.R were in the same billet. This and succeeding days were spent in locating the battalion making some temporary arrangements	
do	2/8/17		"C" Coy of the 2/5th K.L.R moved into the Subsidiary Line of the Coalmine System	
do	3/8/17		"A" & "B" Companies left Bac-St-maur for billets at Rouge -de-Bout	
Rouge de Bout	4/8/17	5.30pm	The G.O.C 57th Division inspected "A" & "B" Companies near Fleurbaix giving a short address complimenting the Battalion on the part they had played in stopping the Enemy over the attack at Ypres on the 31st July	
do	5/8/17		Reinforcements of 1 officer & 5 other ranks arrived	
do	6/8/17		In the early hours of the day the Brigade Major, Capt Alexander was killed by a piece of an aeroplane bomb dropped in Brigade H.Q.	
		5pm	Funeral of Capt Alexander at Sailly. Capt Read (acting CO of 2nd unit) present	
do	7/8/17		Advance parties of the 2/5th & 2/6th K.K.R went to the trenches	
Contemaire	8/8/17	9.30pm	Two companies of the 2/6th K.L.R were attached to this unit. The composite Battalion comprising "A" & "B" Coys of the 2/5th K.L.R & "A" & "B" Coys of the 2/6th K.L.R	

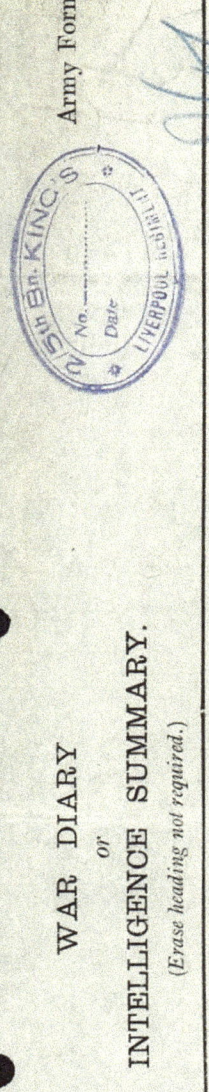

Army Form C. 2118.

WAR DIARY
or
INTELLIGENCE SUMMARY.
(Erase heading not required.)

Instructions regarding War Diaries and Intelligence Summaries are contained in F.S. Regs., Part II. and the Staff Manual respectively. Title pages will be prepared in manuscript.

Place	Date	Hour	Summary of Events and Information	Remarks and references to Appendices
Cordonnerie	9/8/17		under the command of Capt Reed relieved the 2/8th K.L.R. in the Cordonnerie Sub-sector	
do	10/8/17		Everything was quiet on the front row left & right sectors. Enemy bring on the front exceedingly quiet all day	
do	11/8/17	10 pm	Major Liles H.N. arrived back from leave & took command of the Battalion	
do	12/8/17		Everything quiet operations normal.	
do	13/8/17		Yesterdays conditions continued throughout the day	
do	14/8/17		Major W.G.G. Jenkins, 2nd Devonshire Regiment, reported and took command of the 2/6th K.L.R.	
do	13/8/17	1.45pm	The enemy attempted to raid No 1 Post "A" Company at N.8.d.50.95 entering our trenches from stage to the left. Rifle & Lewis Gun Spread fire towards were known. The enemy immediately retired. A second attempt was made by the enemy at 12 midnight on the same post with same results as before.	
do	13/8/17	10.20 pm	The enemy about 15 strong, attempted to raid No 2 Post "A" Company at N.8.d.95.95 but were immediately repulsed. One of the enemy was shot while attempting to climb the parapet, but on search being made only his rifle spark of had	

WAR DIARY
or
INTELLIGENCE SUMMARY.
(Erase heading not required.)

Army Form C. 2118.

Place	Date	Hour	Summary of Events and Information	Remarks and references to Appendices
Cordonnerie	14/8/17	4.30am	equipment was found which had marks of being hit by bullets. Our total casualties in both raids were 1 man slightly wounded. For no apparent reason the enemy opened a barrage on "C" Company sector which lasted until 5.30 am. Our casualties were 1 killed & 4 wounded (all rifleman)	
		5 pm	A British aeroplane brought down in front of our "B" Company sector at about N.14.d central. 2nd Lieut W Smith of "B" Company & 9th Lance Corporal of Kyshaie immediately went out to try to reach the aeroplane which they thought was in No Mans Land. As they were going out they saw a wounded German crawling to the German lines. They immediately captured him & brought him back to our lines & obtained his identity disc & papers. This was done in full view of the enemy, the party having been within 50 yards of the enemy trenches.	
	14/8/17		Sergeant Burke, Corporal Armstrong & Rfm Stokes received cards of recognition for gallant conduct during the shelling of Armentières on the night of 28/29 July	
	15/8/17		Everything quiet during the day	
	16/8/17	4.50 pm.	2/8 K.L.R. relieved us in the Cordonnerie sub sector & the battalion moved	

T./134. Wt. W708—776. 50000. 4/15. Sir J. C. & S.

WAR DIARY
or
INTELLIGENCE SUMMARY.
(Erase heading not required.)

Army Form C. 2118.

Place	Date	Hour	Summary of Events and Information	Remarks and references to Appendices
Rouge de Bout	17/9/17	1.30pm	11/5 Brigade Reserve at Rouge de Bout. Draft of 96 other ranks arrived.	
"	18/9/17	1 pm	Draft of 145 other ranks arrived.	
"	23/9/17		Two officers reported to this Batt for duty.	
Laventie	24/9/17		In the afternoon of this day 2/5th L.R. relieved the 2/4th K.L.R. in the Cordonnerie Subsector.	
"	24/9/17		Reinforcements of 510 other ranks arrived.	

W. Hennessey Capt
Adjutant 2/5th Battn. "The King's" (Liverpool Regt.)

In the Field
30th Sept 1917

Headquarters,
57th Division.

War Diary for the month of September, herewith, please.

W. Humphreys Capt
Adjutant 2/5th Battn. "The King's" (Liverpool Regt.)

Army Form C. 2118.

WAR DIARY or INTELLIGENCE SUMMARY.

(Erase heading not required.)

2/5 Liverpool R

Instructions regarding War Diaries and Intelligence Summaries are contained in F. S. Regs, Part II. and the Staff Manual respectively. Title pages will be prepared in manuscript.

Place	Date	Hour	Summary of Events and Information	Remarks and references to Appendices
CORRDONNERIE	9.9.17	2 PM	Took over from the 2/8th Kings Lpool Regt	
	10.9.17	7 PM	Observed a different enemy regiment in front of us but unable to identify	
	11.9.17	6 AM	Enemy sent over about 80 Wh.B. bangs on our right coy supports. No damage	
	15.9.17	1-30 AM	Enemy put a Barrage on our centre company consisting of Wh.B. bangs & French mortars this he continued until 8-30. Mine fuse was blown in in one place & one man killed & 3 wounded	
	16.9.17	8-20 PM	Relieved by 38th Welsh Division. 13th Battn Welsh. Marched to La Torgu	
	18.9.17	8 AM	Marched to La Perini	
	19.9.17	8-30 AM	Marched to St Hilaire	
St HILAIRE	20.9.17		The Battalion goes into Rest Billets at St HILAIRE & it is anticipated that we shall remain here for 3 weeks. This being the first time that the Unit has been so far back from the time since arriving in France. Syllabus of Work for 1st week includes Range Practice, Musketry, Platoon & Company Drill	
do	30.9.17		Regimental Sports held at St HILAIRE	
			Strength of Battalion on 1.9.17 37 Officers 747 Other ranks 30.9.17 44 do 917 do	Incoming Drafts for month of Sept 2/L all ranks

Adjutant 2/5th Battn. "The King's 8" (Liverpool Regt.)

Army Form C. 2118.

WAR DIARY
or
INTELLIGENCE SUMMARY.
(Erase heading not required.)

2/5 Liverpool Rg.¹ Vol 9.

Place	Date	Hour	Summary of Events and Information	Remarks and references to Appendices
ST HILAIRE	1.10.17		Battalion in Rest Billets.	
—do—	19.10.17	9 AM	Marched from ST HILAIRE to RENESCURE.	
	20.10.17	8 AM	Travelled by Motor Bus from RENESCURE to PROVEN.	
	24.10.17	3.30 P.M.	Trained to ELVERDINGHE.	
	25.10.17		Marched to MARSOUIN FARM. Arrived there at 4.30 p.m. Then in reserve for the night. Weather wet + cold.	
EAGLE TRENCH U23.c. 90.90 @ IXCHOOTE 20.S.W.4.	26.10.17		Left MARSOUIN FARM at 9 p.m. Marched to EAGLE TRENCH + went in support of 2/8 K.L.R. who were holding line approximately V.9 central N.8 D.90.90 V.14.A 10.90 V.14.D 50.90. Company in reserve at V.13.A central. Weather wet. Condition of ground very wet. Two casualties sustained on marching in.	
	27.10.17	12 Noon to 12.30 pm	At noon wet weather ceased. Very little damage done. Companies moved up to the front line from 2/8 K.L.R. Relief finished by 1.30 am. Eight casualties sustained during relief. Disposition of companies: A Co. Right front line, B " Left " ", C " Right support, A " Left "	
	28.10.17	6 p.m.		
		4 A.M. 10 A.M.	Hostile artillery shelled area heavily near time line of Right company. Night-activity high-nor. Weather dull. Condition of ground very bad. Visibility poor. Our artillery barrage enemys front line very heavily during the whole of the afternoon.	
		6 P.M.	2/6 K.L.R. moved up to take over line from us. Relief completed by 2 A.M. during relief we were heavily shelled & also gas. Our casualties on moving out being approximately 70.	
HUDDLESON CAMP D.17.B Central ST JULIEN 28.N.W.2.	29.10.17	3 A.M.	Arrived at HUDDLESON CAMP	
	30.10.17	4.30 pm	Marched from HUDDLESON CAMP to MARSOUIN FARM. The Battalion in Reserve.	
MARSOUIN FARM C.8.B.60.10 ST JULIEN 28.N.W.2.	31.10.17		Battalion in Reserve.	

A. H. Slasher
for O/C 2/5 King's Liverpool Regt.

2/5th The King's Liverpool Regt
In the Field
30/11/17

Headquarters
57th Division

War Diary for November 1917
herewith, please.

J.H. Taylor Capt
for Lieut. Col.
2/5th Bn. "The King's" (L'pool Regt.)

(in absence of C.O & 2nd in Command,
on duty.)

Ends.

WAR DIARY
or
INTELLIGENCE SUMMARY.
(Erase heading not required)

Army Form C. 2118

2/5 Liverpool Vol 10

Instructions regarding War Diaries and Intelligence Summaries are contained in F.S. Regs. Part II. and the Staff Manual respectively. Title pages will be prepared in manuscript.

Place	Date	Hour	Summary of Events and Information	Remarks and references to Appendices
M/ASOUDIN FARM (ST JULIEN 28.N.2 C8.B.6c.10) EAGLE TRENCH U28C.90.90	1/11/17		Battalion in Reserve. Weather misty to clear. Fairly fine.	
		6 pm	Battalion carried line in relief of 2/8 K.L.R who noted the enemy was moving up along "B" track. We encountered heavy shelling on our right near the STEENBEEK. Between relief returned. Weather dull.	
do	1/2/11/17		Very heavy gas shelling during the night. Phosgene & Mustard gas noticeable. Weather dull, foggy.	
	3/11/17 9.30pm		Relieved by 2/10 K.L.R. T marched to WOLFF CAMP. (B.22.D.60.90)	
WOLFF CAMP	3/11/17		Battalion employed on cleaning up generally.	
	4/11/17		do	
	5/11/17		do	
	6/11/17 1 P.M.		Entrained at ELVERDINGHE.	
		7 P.M.	Arrived at AUDRUICQ. Marched into billets at LAPANNE, RECQUE AREA. (FRANCE SHEET 27A N.E J28.A) on relief of 7/8 Battalion by the 62nd Battalion.	
LA PANNE	16/11/17		Battalion used "B" Range with the 2/8th K.L.R.	
do	28/11/17		The following reinforcements arrived during the month. 2 Lt Maylin B.N. 2 Lt Benger G.D., Lt Knight W.F., 2 Lt F. Dawson. and 53 other ranks. (Casualties during the month were Lt. W.B. Kennett (wounded on Nov 2, 1917.) and 11 other ranks.	

J.R. Taylor Capt Lieut-Col
2/5th Bn. "The King's" (L'pool Regt)
In absence of G.O. & Bn in Command
on duty

Army Form C. 2118.

1/5 Liverpool

WAR DIARY
or
INTELLIGENCE SUMMARY.
(Erase heading not required.)

Instructions regarding War Diaries and Intelligence Summaries are contained in F. S. Regs. Part II. and the Staff Manual respectively. Title pages will be prepared in manuscript.

Place	Date	Hour	Summary of Events and Information	Remarks and references to Appendices
LA PANNE	1 DEC		The Battalion was in rest billets managing the usual training	
PROVEN	8 DEC		The unit moved by trains to Portsmouth Camp, Proven where the training was continued	
PROVEN	16 DEC		The Battalion moved forward to Bation Camp, Boesinghe Area as support Battalion	
BOESINGHE	17 DEC 9 PM		The Battalion relieved the 7th Queens Regt 18th Division in the front line opposite Nonthlot Forest and on either side of the Ypres–Staden Railway. "C" + "D" Companies were in the front line. "A" Company in support and "B" Company in reserve at Pascal Farm. Battalion Headquarters were at Egypt House. The relief was carried out without casualties. The four days the battalion was in the line were very quiet.	
	19 DEC 12 MID		"A" Company relieved "D" Company on left front. "B" Company relieved "C" Company who went into reserve "D" Company went into support	
	21 DEC 7:30 AM		The Commanding Officer (Lieut Col M. J. G. Jenkins), whilst visiting the front line posts was wounded by an enemy sniper.	
	21 DEC 8 PM		The 2/8th Batt. Kings X600b Regt relieved this Battalion, who moved back to Bation Camp in support	
	23 DEC 3 AM		Buncanwalker which was in the line were 1 died of wounds 2 wounded (incl. 1 Officer) owing to the bass of two boats by the 2/8th K.L.R. the C+D Companies were with Coyts of the 2/8th K.L.R who had suffered heavy casualties	

WAR DIARY
or
INTELLIGENCE SUMMARY.
(Erase heading not required.)

Army Form C. 2118.

Place	Date	Hour	Summary of Events and Information	Remarks and references to Appendices
BOESINGHE	25 Dec		The Battalion, less "B" & "D" Companies who were in the line, was relieved at Baboon Camp by the 2/4th South Lancashire Regt. The Battalion moved back to Lamey Camp, Elverdinghe, where they were joined at midnight by the two companies who had been in the line.	
ELVERDINGHE	29 Dec		The Battalion moved to Penton Camp, Canada Area, Proven. The move was continued by route march to Les Quatre fils Aymon.	
PROVEN	30 Dec		The move was continued by route march to Waterlands Camp, Meteren.	
METEREN	31 Dec		The move was again continued by route march to Steenwerck.	

W. Henderson Lieut. Col.
2/5th Bn "The King's" (L'pool Regt.)

Army Form C. 2118.

WAR DIARY
or
INTELLIGENCE SUMMARY.
(Erase heading not required.)

Instructions regarding War Diaries and Intelligence Summaries are contained in F. S. Regs., Part II. and the Staff Manual respectively. Title pages will be prepared in manuscript.

Place	Date	Hour	Summary of Events and Information	Remarks and references to Appendices
ARMENTIERES	1/1/18		The Battalion moved into the trenches from WATERLANDS CAMP and relieved the 33rd Bn Australian Infantry Force at Australian Section in the Armentieres Sector.	
	7/1/18		After an extended quiet period in the sector the Battalion was relieved by the 2/8th King's (Liverpool) Regiment and moved into Brigade Reserve at the forward Brasseries.	
	9/1/18		Capt. (A/Major) W Irving-Lane was appointed A Lieut Colonel while commanding the Battalion. Lieut. (A.Capt) G. L. TAYLOR was appointed A MAJOR while acting in absence of Captain	
	12.1.18		During a heavy shelling by the Enemy (ARMENTIERES) a warning came on Anti aircraft post was driven to a shell in a cellar, they were evacuated, after some time and were still at duty time out, uninjured.	
	13.1.18		The battalion moved into Reserve Camp at MENEGATE CAMP	
	17.1.18		The four days were occupied in supplying working parties in dugouts in vicinity of EPROOMZWEN & cable trenches on	
	18.1.18 19.1.18 20.1.18		Three days were then allotted to training which consisted of normal Infantry hour Company Lectures Bayonet &c	
	21.1.18		The battalion moved from MENEGATE CAMP to the ARMENTIERES Sector, relieving the 2/4th East Lancashire Regiment	

2/5th Kings L'pool Regt
In the Field
1.2.1918

Headquarters
57th Division

War Diary for the month of
January 1918, herewith, Please.

[signature] Lieut. Col.
2/5th Bn. "The King's" (L'pool Regt.)

Emy

WAR DIARY
or
INTELLIGENCE SUMMARY.
(Erase heading not required.)

Army Form C. 2118.

2/5 Liverpool Regt

Place	Date	Hour	Summary of Events and Information	Remarks and references to Appendices
ARMENTIERES	24.1.18		After a quiet time in the line the battalion was relieved by the 2/5th K.L.R. on conclusion were 2 killed and 12 wounded, all other ranks. The battalion moved into the training line and relieved the 2/7th K.L.R., Battn Headquarters moved to huts between ARMENTIERES and ERQUINGHEM.	
	27.1.18		The battalion was relieved by the 2/8th K.L.R. in the training line and together with the Battn H.Q. moved into MENEGATE CAMP.	
	31.1.18		While there until the 31st of the month the battalion provided working parties.	
	31.1.18		Orders were received from the Brigade to the effect that the battalion would be distributed among the 2/6 K.L.R. 2/7th K.L.R. 1/8 Bn. and 12th Bn. the Kings Liverpool Regiment under the new organisation scheme. This move would be carried out in the Brigade on 1st February. The personnel moved to the 11th 12th K.L.R. would await orders.	

2/5th Bn. "The Kings" (Liverpool Regt.)

www.ingramcontent.com/pod-product-compliance
Lightning Source LLC
Chambersburg PA
CBHW081503160426
43193CB00014B/2571